Caps

in
felt, knitting and crochet

This book I dedicate to my mother

Olivia

who took care that I - as a child – got a foundation to
have a creative adult life

Caps
in
felt, knitting and crochet

Lis Kruchov Sørensen

Akacia

Translation: Ingerlise Lebech

© 2005 Forlaget Akacia
Skovvænget 1
5690 Tommerup
Denmark
akacia@akacia.dk

Printed at Økotryk I/S, Videbæk, Denmark, 2005

ISBN: 87-7847-084-6

Contents

Introduction

The ancient technique of felting with the enormous possibilities of expression has got a renaissance, and when I some years ago got hold of a lot of leftovers of felt, I found it interesting to combine felt with yarn – and thereby the ideas about the caps arose.

It is an exciting process to felt carded wool in lovely colours, and afterwards it is very relaxing to sit down with a cup of coffee or tea listening to good music and be inspired by the feltpieces, the shape the cap is going to have, which yarns will go with the felt, and finally how the cap could be decorated.

All the caps are mounted with lining so if you want to take a walk or ride your bike on a cold winter day, you are sure to keep your head warm and look smart at the same time.

To produce caps from felt, knitting, and yarn has only given me one problem: it is difficult to stop again. The materials give so many possibilities and combinations that any two caps will never be alike – so take care, you will soon be fascinated – but then you have popular gifts for both family and friends.

Enjoy yourself!

Lis Kruchov Sørensen

Materials

Felt
Carded wool in all the colours of the rainbow

Yarn
Woollen yarn 4 ply and chunky
Sock yarn, Angora,
Chunky multicoloured yarn,
Eyelash yarn, Brushed wool, Mohair

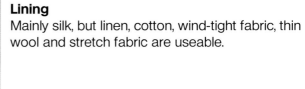

Lining
Mainly silk, but linen, cotton, wind-tight fabric, thin wool and stretch fabric are useable.

Decoration
Yarn of wool, cotton, linen and silk,
felt, beads and sequins.

Basic instructions for felting

Materials
Wool / carded wool
Hot and cold water
Bowl / bucket for water
Whisk and soap flakes
Bubble wrap and mat of bamboo
Vinegar

Felt has opened a new world to me.
From the start I used felt which was made by others. But I had to try on my own and then I was »hooked«. I highly recommend that you start too.

Before you are felting

Measure carded wool into suitable lengths. Beware that it must be twice the length and width as you want the felted fabric to be. Spread the wool into the wanted width. Perhaps you might need twice the length to obtain the width.
Repeat above-mentioned, if wanted with a contrasting colour, and place it at right angles onto the first layer.

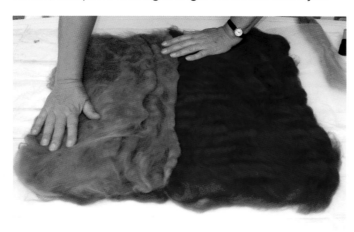

Repeat with the third and fourth layer, arranging the wool cross-ways to the layer below. For thick felt you need five layers of wool. Look for holes and cover with small tuffs of carded wool.

Now for felting

As a rule you are going to use 0.1 ltr of soap flakes for 2½ ltr of boiling water; whip it well. Fill in with cold water till the water is not too hot for your hands. Pour hot soapy water gently over the carded wool and cover with bubble wrap.

Pour a small amount of soapy water over the bubble wrap, so your hands are able to slide. Press with your palms to remove air bubbles out of the wool, at first very gently, later a little harder.

Start felting with gentle motions all over the wrap, at first up and down, later in circles. After a while you can work harder with the felt. Keep rolling the edge of the wool slightly inwards to give it a smooth, finished shape. Add more soapy water while felting, rather too much than too little.

Remove the bubble wrap when the wool holds together. Continue working the felt and add more soapy water.

Work the felt carefully in the beginning. Remember to work the edges carefully. When the fibres are well connected and you have worked all over the area put the felt aside, and spread out the mat on the table. Place the felt on the mat in an even position. Roll the mat tightly round the felt and tie a couple of strings round the rolled up mat.

Take the felt from the mat and shape it into a ball, which you knock down into the table 30 to 50 times.

After-care

The felt is rinsed thoroughly in several changes of tepid water. Remember to add vinegar in the last change of water, which must be cold. Press the water from the felt. Spin and spread the felt on a towel to let it dry. The felt should now be about a third smaller than the piece of carded wool you started out with.

Roll the mat approximately twenty times. Open the mat and turn the felt 90° roll together and repeat the process. Repeat this four times.

Useful information

The caps in this book fit a circumference of head of app. 58 cm (23 ¼ in.).
Basic design E and F mention small circumference which means app. 56 cm (22½ in.). I measure round the head just above the ears.

In the list of materials under the patterns I have mentioned colours of felt and yarn. Naturally you choose the colours, which suit you and your temperament.

When you have to cast off loosely, it is helpful to use a thicker needle to make sure you get an elastic edge. If you use 3 mm, then cast off using needle 5 mm.

When you are mounting the lining it is important to spread it evenly in the cap. Pin it before you stitch it on by hand.

It is sensible to stitch the lining onto the top of the cap with a few stitches.

You will have the best result if you press the work as you go along.

If the cap is going to be decorated it is easier to do this before you knit the lower edge.

When you knit a pattern, it is a good idea to twist the yarns to avoid never-ending floats.

If nothing else is mentioned the templates are in full scale.

Tension/Gauge

If you are not sure about the quality of the yarn, the needles and the tension/gauge it is always a good idea to make a sample.

My tension/gauge:

Wool 4 ply, needle 2 mm – rib
25 stitches = 8 cm

Wool 4 ply, needle 2 mm – stocking stitch
25 stitches = 10,5 cm

Wool 4 ply, needle 3 mm – stocking stitch
25 stitches = 11 cm
30 rows = 11 cm

Wool chunky, needle 6 mm – stocking stitch
15 stitches = 11 cm
19 rows = 11 cm

Wool chunky, crochet hook 6 mm – double crochet
13 stitches = 10 cm

Embroidery stitches

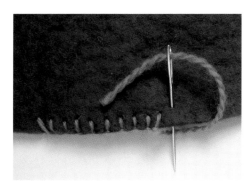

Blanket stitches
I use when sewing round the feltpieces. I join the feltpieces in the blanket stitches and I pick up stitches in them.

Stem stitches
I use for stems and setting off the lines of the felt.

Chain stitches
I use to mark lines in the feltpieces

Back stitches
I use to mark the lines of the felt, for flowerstems and especially for "stardust" as decoration.

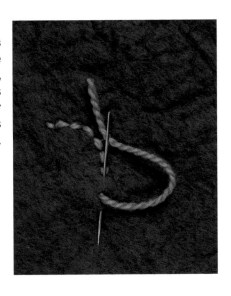

Lazy Daisy
I use to spread flowers in many colours on the feltpieces.

French knots
I often use for decoration with beads.

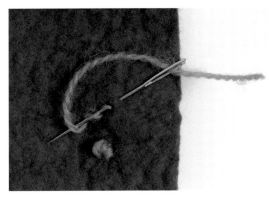

11

Anna

Basic Design A

You can turn the edge up or down – depending on your mood.
The felt flower can be placed on the cap, or you can use it as decoration on a jacket or a handbag.

Materials
35 x 60 cm (14 x 24 in.) of felted fabric (mixture in grey)
A small amount of woollen yarn, 4 ply (light grey)
25 x 60 cm (10 x 24 in.) of lining

Hem

Join the piece of felt at the short end into a tube. Fold double (4cm, 1½ in.). Join crown and hem. Sew through the three layers of blanket stitches.

Crown

Cut 5 pieces of felt, according to the template on page 15.
Cut a piece of felt measuring 8 x 60 cm (3 ¼ x 24 in.) for hem.
Sew blanket stitches round every piece of felt (max ½ cm (¼ in) between stitches)

The crown is sewn together in this way: Place 2 pieces of felt, right sides together.
Sew through both layers in the blanket stitches along the length of one side.

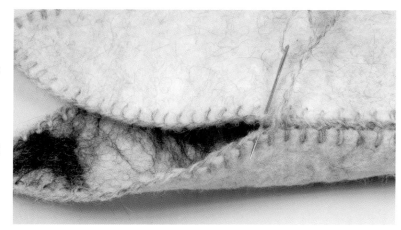

Mounting the lining

Cut lining according to the template on page 15. Allow 1 cm (½ in.) for seam allowance.

Fold out the pieces and place another piece of felt, right sides together. Continue making up all 5 pieces.

Join the lining on sewing machine. Pin the lining to the hat, just above the hem, and stitch it on by hand.

Flower of felt

You can make a flower like the model, but you can also choose to make flowers of felt from your own ideas - no flowers will be alike.

Materials
Leftovers of felt (red, yellow and green shades)
Beads
Safety-pin for a brooch

Cut pieces of felt, according to template on page 15.

1.Pin the flower to the leaves.

2. Place the centerpiece on the flower and join all layers at the same time as you sew on beads.

3. Turn around the flower and sew on the back, covering the stitches.

4. Mount the safety-pin.

Anna – template

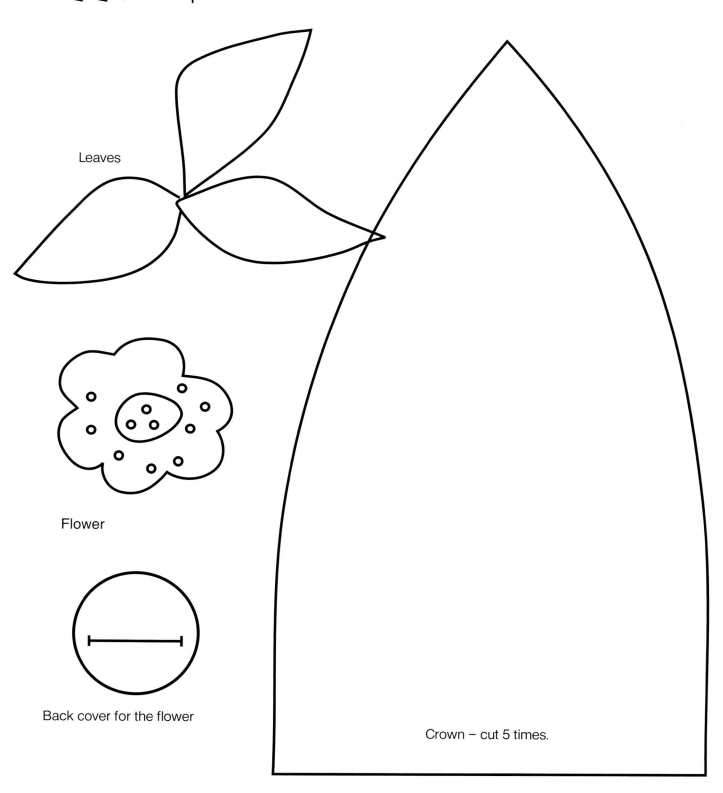

Leaves

Flower

Back cover for the flower

Crown – cut 5 times.

Basic Design A

Here you have a felt cap which has become even more sophisticated with its edge of rabbitfur. It will keep your ears warm.

Mounting of lining and fur

Cut lining according to the template on page 15.
Beware of 1 cm (½ in.) for seam allowance.
Join the lining on sewing machine.
Pin the lining to the cap.
Place the fur on the cap, right sides together, and sew on sewing machine, through felt, lining and fur, with 1 cm (½ in.) for seam allowance.

Crown

Cut 5 pieces of felt according to the template on page 15.
Sew blanket stitches along the sides, (max ½ cm (¼ in) between stitches). Do not sew the lower edge.
Join the crown according to page 13.

Bend the fur to wrong side so the width is halved add padding for more fullness. Stitch the hem of fur to the lining by hand, using a needle for leather and double thread.

Edging

Measure the lower circumference of the cap and match the edge of fur.
Join the fur at the short side and sew on sewing machine.

Basic Design A

If you ride a bike a lot, this cap with its ear flaps will be perfect. You might want to crochet tiestrings so the cap fits tightly when tied

Materials
30 x 60 cm (12 x 24 in) of felt (blue shades)
A small amount of woollen yarn, 4 ply, (navy)
A small amount of eyelash yarn (cobalt)
30 x 60 cm (12 x 24 in.) of lining.
Crochet hook 3 mm
Beads for decoration

Agate

Crown

Cut 3 pieces of felted fabric according to the template on page 15. Cut 2 pieces of felted fabric according to the pattern on page 20.
Sew blanket stitches (max ½ cm, (¼ in.) between stitches) round the pieces of felt.
Join the pieces of felt in this way:

Place piece number 1 and piece number 2, right sides together and sew along one side through both layers of blanket stitches.
Fold out the felt and join piece number 3 with number 2, right sides together. Join all 5 pieces. Beware of the ear flaps (piece number 1 and 3), they have different roundings forward and backward.

Decoration

Decoration of the cap.
I have used 4 mm beads in dark metallic shades, but any beads can be used.
Sew the beads on pieces number 4 and 5 or spread them all over the cap.

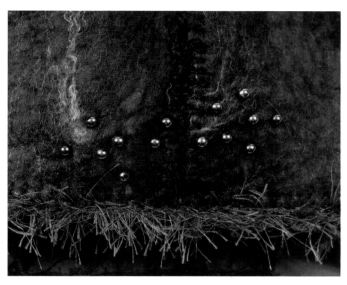

Mounting of lining

Cut lining according to the templates on page 15 and 20. Allow 1 cm (½ in.) for seam allowance.
Join the lining on sewing machine according to the instructions for crown.
Pin the lining to the cap and stitch it on by hand.
Make 1 row of doubble crochet (US single crochet) with eyelash yarn. Crochet in the blanket stitches.

Agate – template

Set the copying machine to 125%

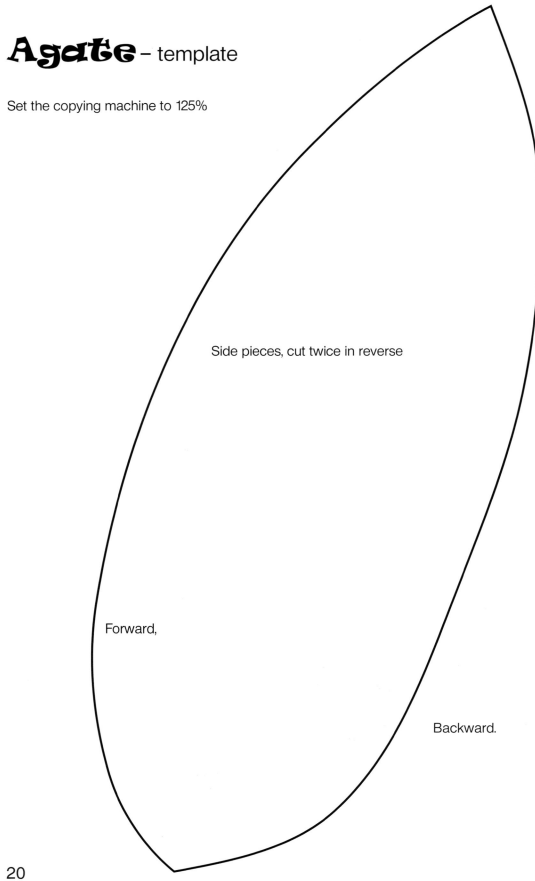

Side pieces, cut twice in reverse

Forward,

Backward.

20

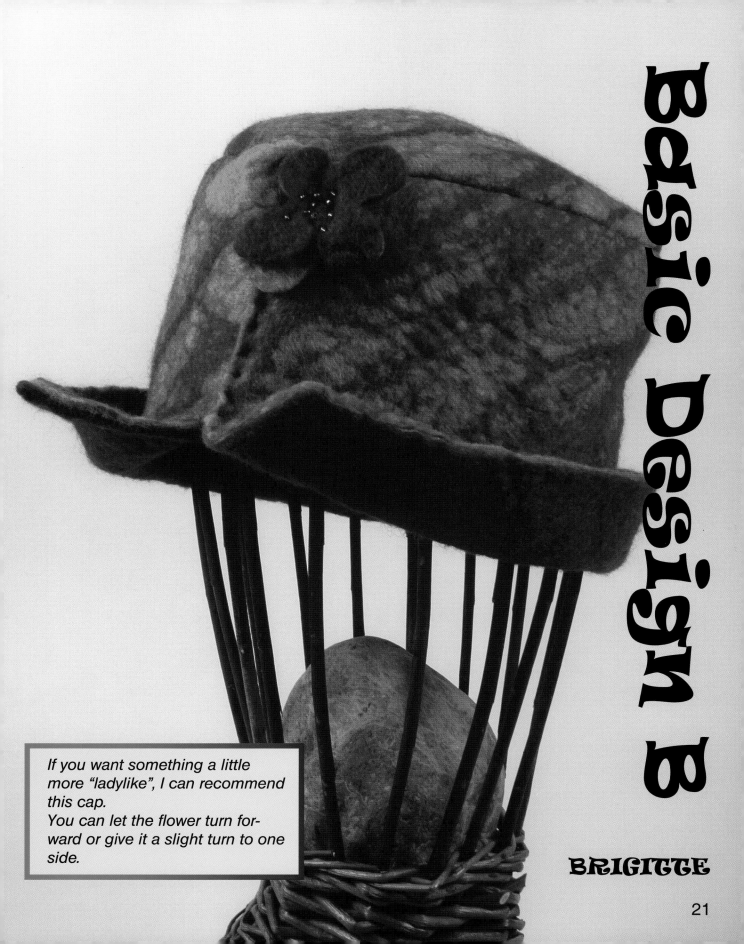

Basic Design B

If you want something a little more "ladylike", I can recommend this cap.
You can let the flower turn forward or give it a slight turn to one side.

BRIGITTE

BRIGITTE

Mounting the hat

Join the feltpiece into a tube by putting the straight side underneath the side with the flower, with 1 cm (½ in.) for seam allowance, and pin it.

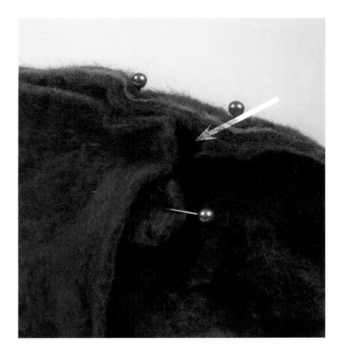

Place lower edge of pattern on lower edge of felt, draw up left side and cut.

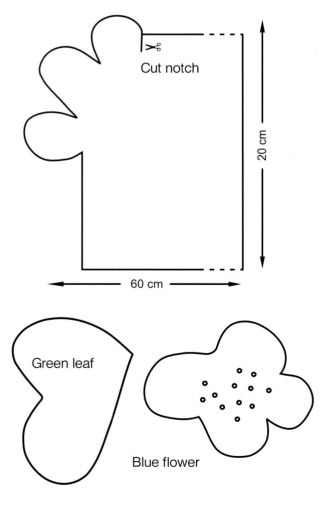

Cut notch

20 cm

60 cm

Green leaf

Blue flower

Turn out the wrong side of the tube and pin it onto the circle so the circumference fits. Beware that the upper leaf is bent towards the right side of the cap to prevent it from being sewn into the seam. The straight side just has to reach the notch at the flower.

Sew on sewing machine with 1 cm (½ in.) for seam allowance.
Cut a notch in the seam allowance for every 5 cm (2 in.)
Turn inside out, and sew with "invisible" stitches by

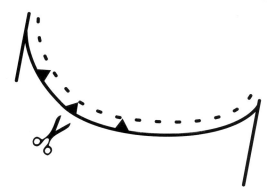

hand, from the flower along the side till 7 cm (2 ¾ in.) before lower edge, which has to be open for hem.

Mounting of lining
Cut lining according to the circle on page 52 and a part measuring 15 x 60 cm (6 x 24 in.)
Join the lining on sewing machine.
Bend seam allowance so that the lower 7 cm (2 ¾ in.) of the hat is without lining.
Pin the lining and stitch it on by hand.

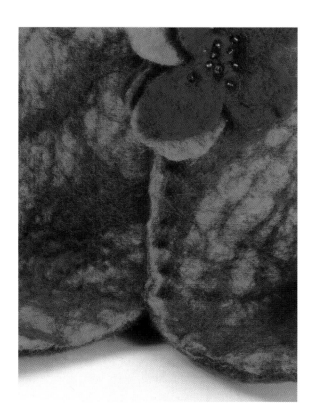

Pin the leaf and flower on the flower of felt, sew by hand and sew on beads at the same time.

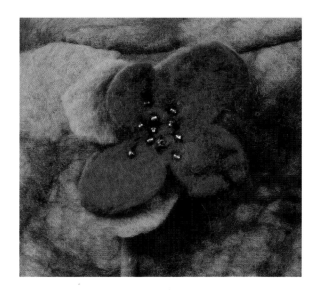

23

Carol

Basic Design C

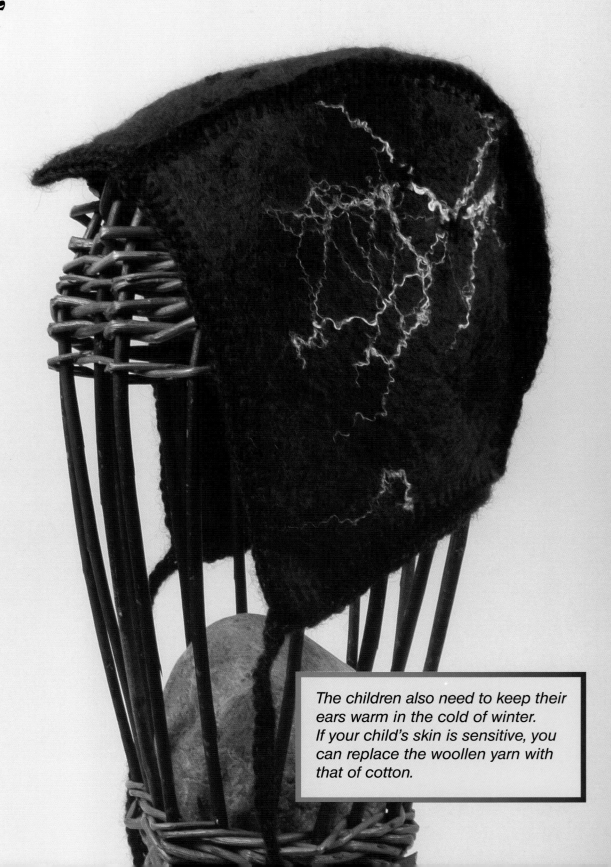

The children also need to keep their ears warm in the cold of winter.
If your child's skin is sensitive, you can replace the woollen yarn with that of cotton.

Materials
35 x 45 cm (14 x18 in.) of felted fabric (blue
and green shades with white silk threads.)
10 gram woollen yarn 4 ply (navy)
40 x 50 cm (16 x 20 in.) of lining
Crochet hook 3 mm.

Helmet

Cut pieces of felt according to the template on page
26. Beware that the 2 side pieces are cut 1 in reverse.
Sew blanket stitches round the pieces of felt. (Max ½
cm, (¼ in.) between stitches)
Place the pieces of felt, wrong side together, and
double crochet (US single crochet) through the blanket
stitches.

Continue to left point of ear flap. Make a string.
Make an extra row of double crochet (US single
crochet) along the lower edge.

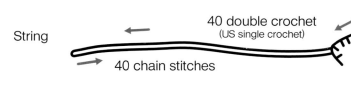

String

40 double crochet
(US single crochet)

40 chain stitches

back

side

start

Crochet a row of double crochet (US single crochet)
round the helmet, begin at the point of left ear flap.

Crochet through the blanket stitches along lower edge.
Crochet 40 chain stitches at the point of right ear flap
for string, turn and crochet 40 double crochet. (US
single crochet)

Mounting of lining

Cut lining with 1 cm (½ in.) for seam allowance
according to the template on page 26. Join the lining on
sewing machine. Pin the lining to the helmet and stitch
it on by hand.
Stitch, if necessary, the lining a few times, so it is
correctly positioned.

Continue to the point in front of the helmet.

Crochet 3 double crochet
(US single crochet)
in the blanket stitch for rounding.

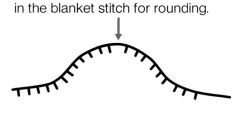

Carol – template

Set the copying machine for 125%

Centre piece
Cut once

Side piece.
Cut 2 pieces 1 in reverse.

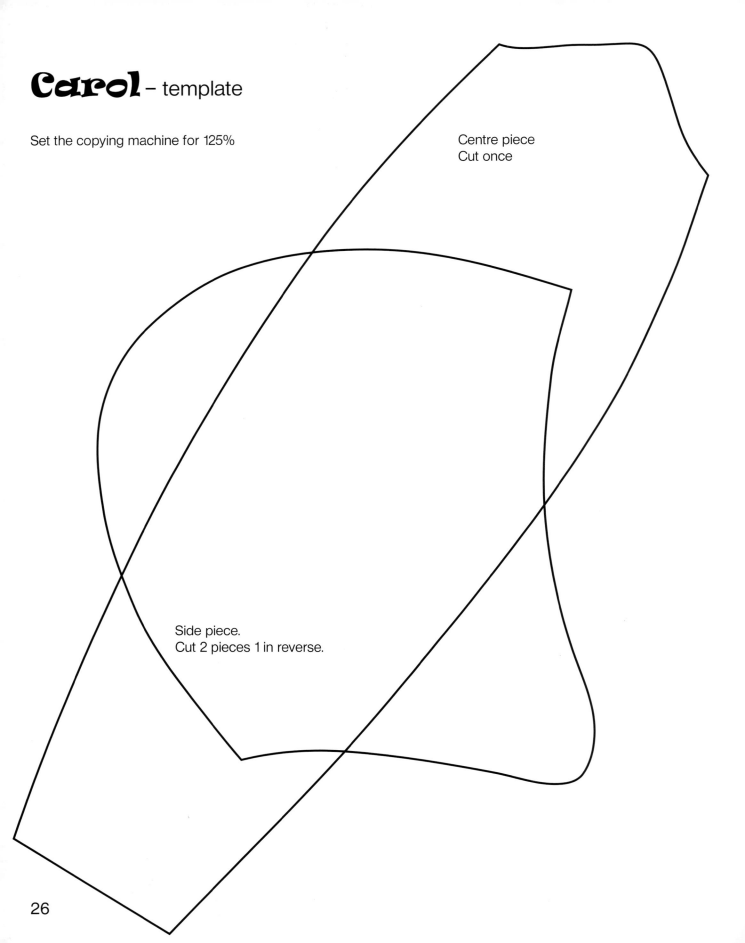

Basic Design D

DIANA

You may not think this cap looks easy to make, but just follow the instruction step by step, and you will end up with a lovely cap.

Crown

Cut 5 pieces of felt, according to the template on page 30.

Sew blanket stitches (max ½ cm (¼ in.) between stitches) round every piece of felt.

Knitting

Start off with one of the felted pieces. Pick up 3 stitches on double-pointed needles in the head of the cut. Knit stocking stitch.

On the rightside, pick up 1 stitch in the first and last blanket stitch. (increasing)

Measure if you have to pick up in every or every other blanket stitch.

Continue in this way to the top. (19 stitches)
Transfer the stitches to the circular needle and place a marker
Repeat this on the other four pieces.
Join and knit 2 rows. (5x19 stitches)
Following makes decreases on every second row, above every marker.
Slip 1 stitch, knit 2 together, pass slipped stitch over .
Change to double-pointed needles when necessary.
Continue decreasing to 15 stitches remaining.
Next row: knit 2 stitches together all over.
Cast off and weave in the ends.

Join the pieces of felt, right sides together by overcasting through the blanket stitches.

Decoration
Embroider flowers and leaves all over, using Lazy Daisy stitches.

Lower edge
Is made up of a border of Jacquard, double rolling edge and a hem inside the cap.

Jacquard
Pick up 120 stitches in the blanket stitches, using circular needle 3 mm and denim yarn. Knit 10 rows from chart. (3 cm, 1 ¼ in.)

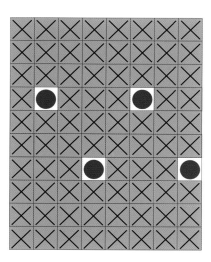

Double rolling edge
Change to circular needle 2 mm and cobalt yarn. Knit 3 cm (1 ¼ in.) of stocking stitch and cast off loosely.
Knit the second rolling edge in this way:
Pick up 120 stitches using circular needle 2 mm, this time on the inside of the cap. Pick up the loops of purl stitches, where you started to knit (3 cm, 1 ¼ in.).
Knit 4 cm, (1½ in.) stocking stitch. Cast off loosely.

Edge inside the cap
Once again pick up 120 stitches using circular needle 2 mm inside the cap. Pick up in the purl stitches like before.
Knit 3 cm, (1 ¼ in.) stocking stitch and cast off loosely.
Stitch the hem to the inside of the cap, covering the Jacquard knitting.

Mounting of lining
Cut 5 pieces of lining according to the template on page 39. Allow 1 cm, (½ in.) for seam allowance.
Join the lining on sewing machine.
Pin the lining to the cap, and stitch it on by hand.

DIANA – template

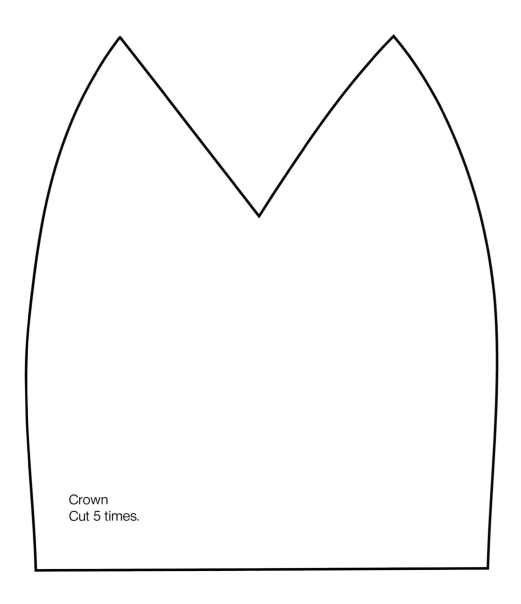

Crown
Cut 5 times.

Basic Design D

DEBORAH

This cap looks peasantlike with lovely flowers and leaves made from felt.

Materials

15 x 65 cm (6 x 26 in.) of felted fabric (bordeaux, lilac and pink shades).
Leftovers of felt for decoration (green, blue and orange shades)
50 gram woollen yarn, 4 ply (bordeaux and green)
25 x 80 cm (10 x 32 in.) of lining.
Circular needles 2 and 3 mm (40 cm, 16. in)
Double-pointed needles 3 mm.

Hem

Pick up 120 stitches in blanket stitches along the lower edge, using circular needle 2 mm and bordeaux yarn. Knit 3 cm, (1 ¼ in.) stocking stitch. Knit 1 row of purl. Knit 3 cm, (1 ¼ in.) stocking stitch. Cast off loosely. Bend 3 cm (1 ¼ in.) to the wrong side and stitch it loosely on by hand.

Crown

Make the crown according to the instruction for Basic Design D - Diana on page 27

Decoration

The decoration of felt is made before the edge is knitted.
Cut flowers and leaves according to the template on page 33

The flowers are embroidered with woollen yarn and back stitches. The stem is embroidered with stem stitches.
Refer to embroidery stitches on page 11.

Mounting of lining

Cut 5 pieces of lining according to the template on page 39. Allow 1 cm, ½ in. for seam alowance.
Join the lining on sewing machine.
Pin the lining to the cap and stitch it on by hand.

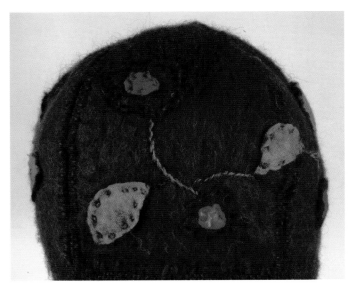

DEBORAH – template

Dorthe

Basic Design D

Flowers and beads spread over this warm cap with ear flaps. The reflections of light in the beads give life to the dark felt.

Materials

Dorthe

30 x 65 cm (12 x 26 in.) of felted fabric (navy, pink, blue and green shades)
100 gram woollen yarn, 4 ply, (dark lilac)
A small amount of eyelash yarn (dark lilac)
40 x 80 cm (16 x 32 in.) of lining.
Circular needles 2mm and 3mm (40 cm, 16 in.)
Double-pointed needles 3mm
Crochet hook 3 mm
Beads for decoration.

Crown

Cut 3 pieces of felt according to the template on page 30
Cut 2 pieces of felt according to the template on page 36
Continue as described at model Diana on page 28
The ear flaps are placed as described at model Agnete on page 18.

Decoration

Embroider flowers with Lazy Daisy and spread the beads so they draw the outlines of the felt.
Refer to embroidery stitches on page 11

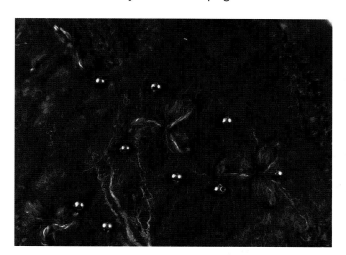

Mounting of lining

Cut pieces of lining as described for the crown, allow 1 cm, ½ in for seam allowance.
Join the lining on sewing machine.
Pin the lining to the cap and stitch it on by hand.

Edge

After the cap is knitted and joined, crochet 1 row of double crochet (US single crochet) with eyelash yarn in the blanket stitches all along the lower edge.

Dorthe – template

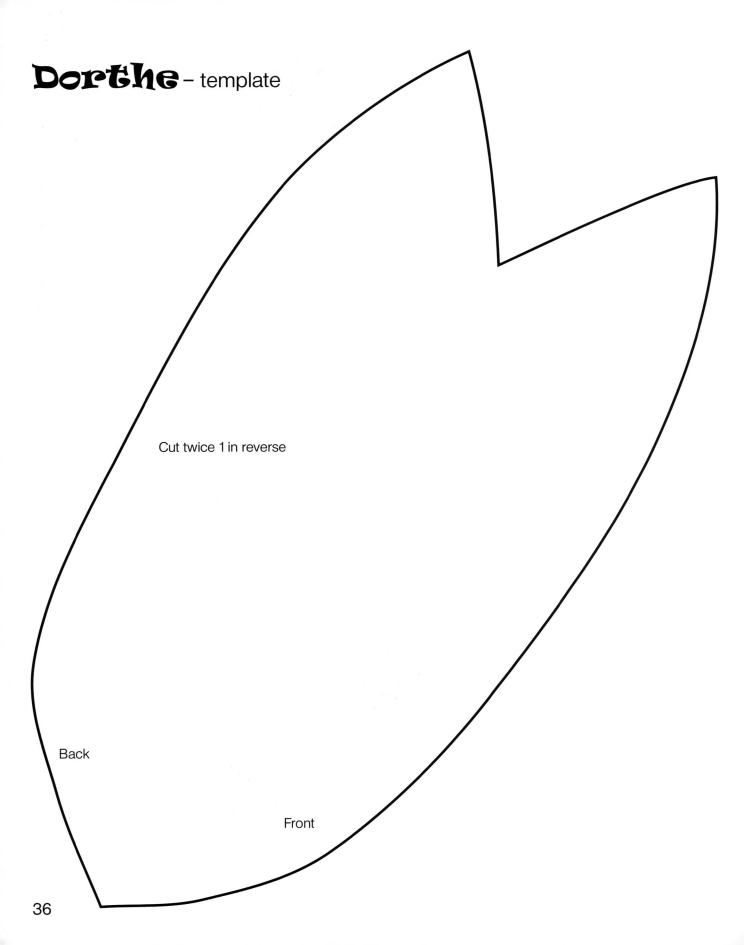

Cut twice 1 in reverse

Back

Front

Basic Design E

Eva

For this cap I have used eyelash yarn and beads which make the cap really festive.

Materials
25 x 45 cm (10 x 18 in.) of felted fabric (bordeaux, orange and lime shades).
50 gram woollen yarn, 4 ply (bordeaux)
50 gram eyelash yarn (winered)
25 x 80 cm (10 x 32 in.) of lining
Circular needle 2 and 3 mm (40 cm, 16 in.)
Double-pointed needles 3 mm
Beads

Eva

Crown

Cut 3 pieces of felt according to the template on page 39

Knitting

Knit 3 pieces in this way:

Cast on 25 (30) stitches, using double-pointed needles 3 mm and woollen yarn. (25 stitches are for a small circumference of head. See page 10)

Knit 7 cm (2 ¾ in) stocking stitch. On every 4th and 5th row, knit with eyelash yarn and woollen yarn together.

Decrease 1 stitch in the beginning and the end of right side rows, until 10 stitches remain.

Decrease every other right side row – measure meanwhile. The knitted work must measure the same lengthwise as the felt.

Cast off, when 3 (4) stitches remain.

Sew blanket stitches round the 3 felted pieces, (max ½ cm, ¼ in. between stitches).

Join the 6 pieces, alternating piece of knitting and piece of felt, right sides together. Sew in the blanket stitches of the felt.

Decoration

Sew on beads all along the lower edge.

Hem

Pick up 120 stitches, using circular needles 3 mm and woollen yarn, at the lower edge of the cap. Pick up in both knitted and felted pieces.

Knit 4 cm, 1½ in stocking stitch. On every other row knit with both woollen and eyelash yarn.

Knit 1 row purl for bending.

Change to circular needles 2 mm and knit 4 cm, 1½ in. stocking stitch with woollen yarn.

Cast off loosely and bend the hem to wrong side and stitch it loosely to the cap.

Mounting of lining

Cut 6 pieces of lining according to the template on page 39. Allow 1 cm, ½ in. for seam allowance. Join the lining on sewing machine. Pin the lining to the cap and stitch it on loosely by hand.

Eva – template

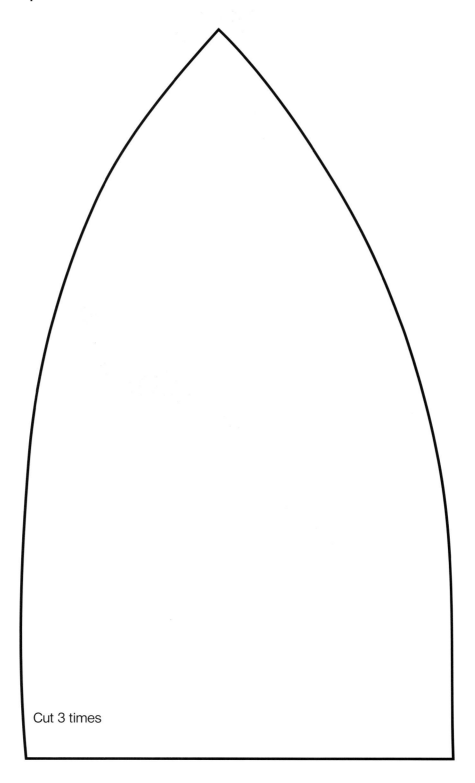

Cut 3 times

Freja

Basic Design F

This pointy cap is becoming for most heads, and the colours grey and black are suitable for most outdoor things.

Crown

Cut 3 pieces of felt according to the template on page 43

Knitting

Knit 3 pieces in this way:
Cast on 25 (30) stitches using double-pointed needles 3 mm. (25 stitches for small circumference of head.)
Knit 5 cm (2 in.) stocking stitch
Decrease 1 stitch in both sides on every other right side row, until remaining 3 stitches.
Measure meanwhile, the knitted piece must be 3 cm (1 ¼ in) shorter than the felted piece.
Cast off.

Sew blanket stitches round the felted pieces (max ½ cm (¼ in.) between stitches).
Join the 6 pieces, right sides together, alternating felt and knit.
Sew in the blanket stitches.

Sew the top in this way.

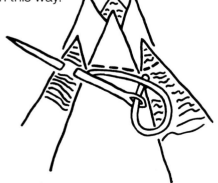

Decoration

Embroider small »stars«, using back stitches and beads spread over the felted pieces.

Hem

The hem is made up of a border of Jacquard, double rolling edge and a hem inside the cap. Refer to page 42.

Jacquard

Pick up 120 stitches in the blanket stitches at the lower edge, using circular needle 3 mm and grey yarn. Knit 4 cm (1½ in.) from chart.

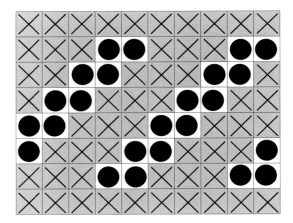

Double rolling edge

Change to circular needle 2 mm and knit 8 rows. Cast off loosely.
Pick up 120 stitches using circular needle 2 mm and black yarn inside the cap. Pick up the loops of purl stitches, right where you started the other rolling edge. Knit 10 rows of stocking stitch.
Cast off loosely.

Hem inside the cap

Pick up 120 stitches using circular needle 2 mm and black yarn right at the start of the rolling edges an knit 4 cm (1½ in.) stocking stitch. Cast off loosely.
Stitch the hem to the inside of the cap by hand, covering the Jacquard border.

Mounting of lining

Cut the lining according to the template – Design E – Eva on page 39
Join the lining on sewing machine.
Pin the lining to the cap and stitch it on by hand above the hem.

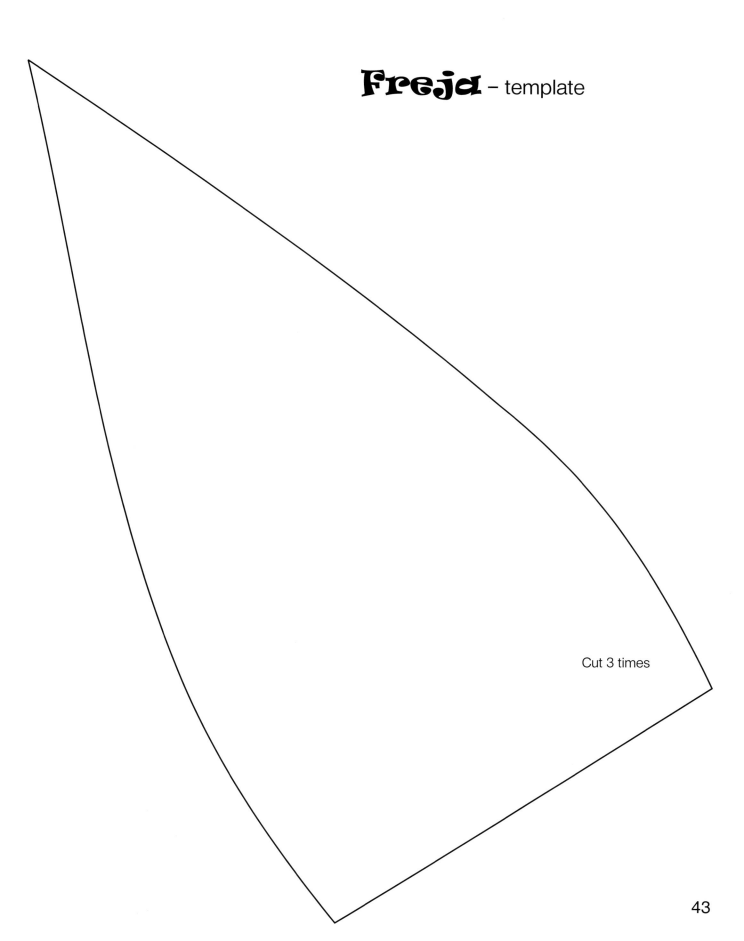

Freja – template

Cut 3 times

43

Basic Design F

Fanny

If you have not got plaits yourself, you can make them on your cap. In case you want thicker plaits, you can crochet more thrums into the work.

Materials

Fenny

25 x 40 cm (10 x 16 in.) of felted fabric (black and grey shades)
50 gram chunky woollen yarn (grey)
50 gram multicoloured sock yarn
30 x 70 cm (12 x 28 in.) of lining
Circular needle 3 and 6 mm (40 cm, 16 in.)
Double-pointed needles 6 mm
Crochet hook 6 mm.

Crown

Cut 3 pieces of felt according to the template for Basic Design F – Freja on page 43.
Sew blanket stitches, (max. ½ cm ¼ in. between stitches), round the felted pieces.

Knitting

Knit 3 pieces in this way:
Cast on 15 stitches, using double-pointed needle 6 mm with grey chunky yarn and sock yarn together.
Knit 8 rows of stocking stitch.
Decrease 1 stitch in beginning of next 2 rows. # Knit 4 rows, decrease at the beginning of next 2 rows #.
Repeat # - # 5 times.

Remaining 3 stitches. Now you start the braids by crocheting the remaining 3 stitches together to one stitch. Make 20 chain stitches. Cut the yarn with an end (3 cm, 1 ¼ in.) and pull it through. Tighten and make a knot.

Join the 6 pieces, right sides together, alternating felt and knit. Sew in the blanket stitches. Join the top, using double yarn, refering to page 41.

Hem

Pick up 80 stitches at the lower edge, using circular needle 6 mm.
Knit 8 rows of stocking stitch.
Purl 1 row
Change to circular needle 3 mm and knit 8 rows.
Cast off loosely.
Bend the hem to wrong side and stitch it loosely on by hand.

Mounting of lining

Cut and sew the lining as descibed for Basic Design F – Freja on page 42.

Basic Design F

If you like long points, parties and colours, this cap will be just right. The fresh combination of colours makes the cap quite unique.

Materials

40 x 40 cm (16 x 16 in.) of felted fabric
(turquoise and lilac shades)
50 gram woollen yarn, 4 ply. (dark lilac)
50 gram eyelash yarn (dark lilac)
30 x 80 cm (12 x 32 in.) of lining.
Circular needle 2 and 3 mm (40 cm, 16 in.)
Double-pointed needles 3 mm

Crown

Cut 3 pieces of felt according to the template on page 48

Knitting

Knit 3 pieces in this way:
Cast on 30 stitches, using woollen yarn and double-pointed needles 3 mm
Knit 7 cm (2 ¾ in.) stocking stitch in this way: 2 rows with woollen yarn, 2 rows with woollen yarn and eyelash yarn together.
Decrease 1 stitch at the beginning and the end of every other right side row. (the row knitted with woollen yarn)
Continue until 4 stitches are remaining and the piece measures 20 cm (8 in.)
Cast off.
Sew blanket stitches, (max ½ cm, ¼ in. between stitches), round the felted pieces.
Join the felt- and knitted pieces alternately, right sides together.
Join the top as shown on page 41.

Decoration
Embroider stars using back stitch and woollen yarn, spread all over the felted pieces.

Hem

Pick up 120 stitches in the felted and the knitted pieces, at the lower edge of the cap, using circular needle 3 mm.
Knit 4 cm (1½ in) alternating wool and eyelash yarn.
Purl 1 row
Change to circular needle 2 mm. Knit 4 cm (1½ in) stocking stitch with woollen yarn for bending.
Cast off loosely.
Stitch the hem loosely to the inside of the cap by hand.

Mounting of lining

Cut and join as described for Basic Design F – Freja on page 42

47

Fie – template

Crown.
Cut 3 times

Lengthen with 5 cm (2 in.)

Basic Design G

This cap has a small edge in patterned knitting.
You can also choose patterned knitting for all of the knitted part by repeating the pattern.

Gretha

Gretha

Materials
20 x 20 cm (8 x 8in.) of felted fabric (denim, bordeaux, lilac and grey shades)
60 gram woollen yarn, 4 ply (dark denim)
20 x 80 cm (8 x 32 in.) of lining
Circular needle 2 and 3 mm (40 cm, 16 in.)

Crown
The crown is made of a circular piece of felt and a knitted part.

Felt
Cut the piece of felt according to the template on page 52
Sew 120 blanket stitches round the felt with max ½ cm (¼ in.) between the stitches.

Decoration
Outline the crossing between the shades of the felt. Embroider stem stitches, using woollen yarn in one of the shades of the felt or choose a contrasting colour

Knitting
Pick up 120 stitches in the blanket stitches, using circular needle 3 mm. Start at the middle of the back. Knit 5 cm (2 in.) stocking stitch.

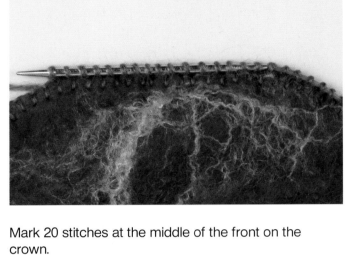

Mark 20 stitches at the middle of the front on the crown.

Knit to the first mark, turn and purl to the second mark. Knit 1 row – all stitches #. Repeat # - # 3 more times.
Knit all stitches till the back of the crown measures 13 cm (5 ¼ in.) where it is highest.

50

Edge

The edge is made up of a border of Jacquard knitting, rolling edge and a hem inside the cap.

The border of Jacquard
Knit by chart.

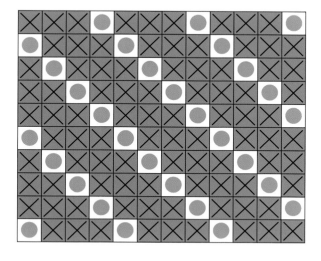

Hem inside the cap

Pick up 120 stitches, using circular needle 2 mm, right where you started the rolling edge. Pick up in purl loops inside the cap.
Knit 3 cm (1 ¼ in.) stocking stitch and cast off loosely.
Stitch the hem to the inside of the cap.

Mounting of lining

Cut lining according to the template on page 52 and a piece measuring 15 x 60 cm (6 x 24 in.). Allow 1 cm (½ in.) for seam allowance.

Rolling edge

Change after the border to circular needle 2 mm and knit 8 rows.
Cast off loosely.

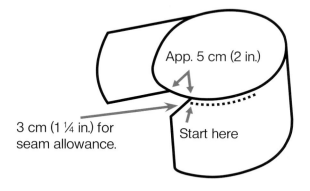

Start joining the pieces app. 3 cm (1 ¼ in.) inside the straight piece of lining.
Sew round the circle until 5 cm (2 in.) remain. Check the circumference. Join the straight piece of lining lengthwise. Sew the remaining piece of the circle.
Pin the lining to the cap above the hem and stitch it on by hand.

Gretha - template

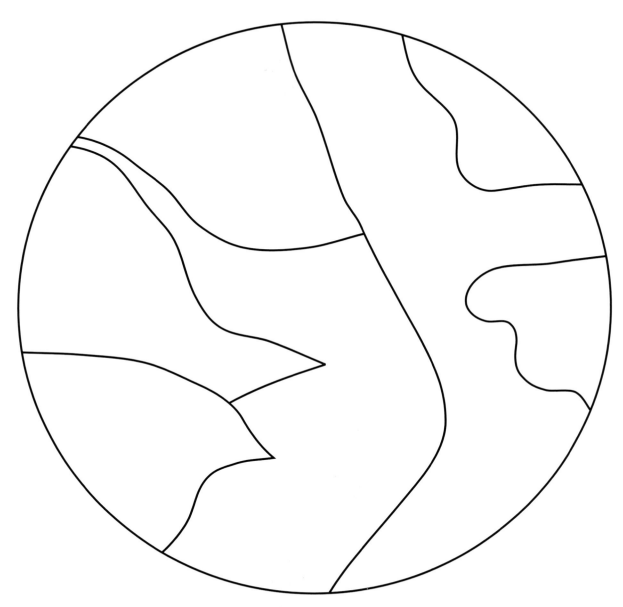

Set the copying machine for 125 %

Diameter 20 cm

Basic Design G

The bouclé yarn used for this cap I found in a basket outside a shop selling yarn. It goes well with eyelash yarn in a lighter shade of red.

Gudrun

Materials

20 x 20 cm (8 x 8 in.) of felted fabric (wine-red)
60 gram woollen yarn (winered boucle)
A small amount of eyelash yarn (red)
20 x 80 cm (8 x 32 in.) of lining
Circular needle 2 and 3 mm (40 cm, 16 in.)
Beads

Edge

Knit 3 cm (1 ¼ in.) stocking stitch alternating 1 row of woollen yarn and 1 row of eyelash yarn, using circular needle 3 mm.
Knit 1 row of holes in this way.
yarn over, knit 2 stitches together #. Repeat # - # throughout the row.
Change to circular needle 2 mm and bouclé yarn. Knit 3 cm (1 ¼ in) stocking stitch
Cast off loosely
Bend the hem at the row of holes and stitch it to the inside of the cap by hand.

Crown

The crown is made of one circular piece of felt and a knitted part.

Felt

Cut the felt according to the template on page 55.
Sew blanket stitches round the felt with max ½ cm (¼ in.) between stitches.

Decoration

Decorate the circle of felt as illustrated on page 55, or use your imagination.
Choose bouclé yarn and embroider flowers using Lazy Daisy.

Knitting

Knit the crown as described for Basic Design G – Gretha on page 50. However, without border of Jacquard.

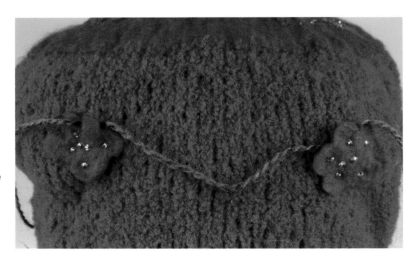

A little extra decoration on the crown

Cut 2 irregular flowers of felt. Sew the small flowers onto the cap with beads, placed where the contrasting yarn marks 20 stitches in the middle of front.

Mounting of lining

Cut and sew the lining as described for Basic Design G – Gretha on page 51.

Gudrun – template

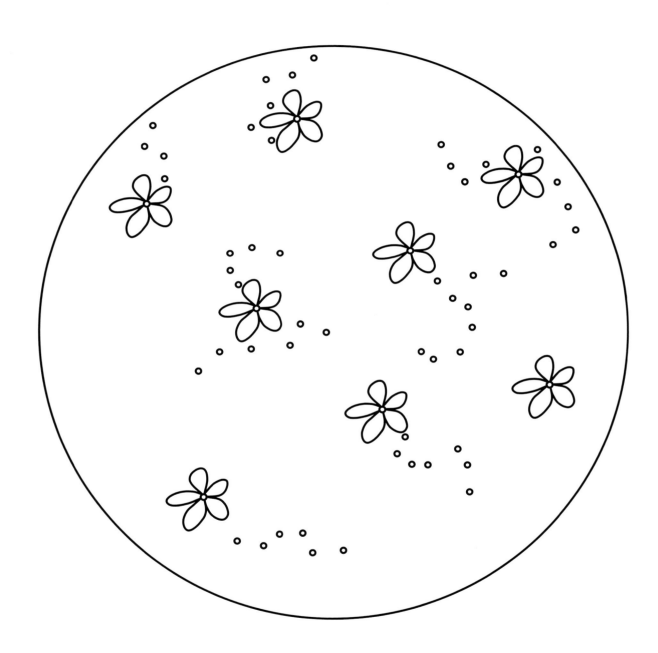

Set the copying machine for 125 %

Diameter 20 cm

Basic Design G

It is quick to crochet in thick yarn. The cap gets a different look because the felt is split into four parts and the crocheted part is made forwards and backwards. The edge looks nice turned up as well as down.

Materials
20 x 20 cm (8 x 8 in.) of felted fabric
(natural white and camel shades)
100 gram chunky woollen yarn and
50 gram brushed woollen yarn and
20 gram woollen yarn, 4 ply, all natural
white
Woollen yarn for embroidery
25 x 25 cm (10 x 10 in.) of lining
Crochet hooks 3 mm and 6 mm
Beads.

Crown

The crown is made of a circular piece of felt, cut in four pieces – and a crocheted part.

Felt

Cut 4 pieces of felt according to the template on page 58
Sew with woollen yarn, 4 ply, blanket stitches round

the pieces of felt. (Max. ½ cm, ¼ in. between stitches) Join by overcasting in the blanket stitches so the pieces of felt form a circle. There must be a total of 90 blanket stitches round the circle.

Decoration

Decorate the felt with stars in back stitches as illustrated on template on page 58.

Crochet

Start crochet in the middle of the back.
Do double crochet (US single crochet)
1. row: # Double crochet in 3 blanket stitches, skip 1 blanket stitch #. Repeat # - # throughout the row. (68 double crochet stitches)
2. row: # Double crochet 5 stitches, skip 1 stitch #. Repeat # - # throughout the row. (60 double crochet stitches)
Continue doing 60 double crochet till the crown measures 10 cm (4 in.)

Mark with contrasting yarn (orange) 12 stitches in the middle of the front.
Crochet till first mark, turn and crochet back to second mark. Turn and crochet till 1 stitch before the first mark, make a new mark. Turn and crochet to 1 stitch before the second mark, make a new mark here. Turn and crochet till 5 stitches before the first mark, make a new mark here. Turn and crochet back till 5 stitches before the second mark, make a new mark here.
Turn and crochet till 1 stitch before the first mark, make a new mark here. Turn and crochet back till 1 stitch before the second mark, make a new mark here.# Repeat # - # one more time.
The four orange marks, illustrated on the picture, are now done.

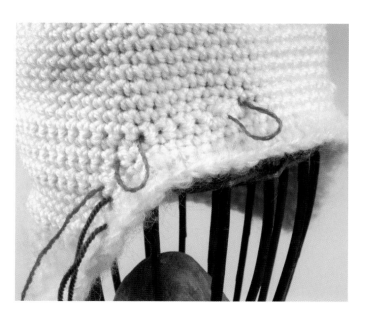

The blue marks illustrated on the picture:
To make a rounding you crochet 2 rows. Do 2 stitches in every point of the »corners«
The blue marks are now done.
Change to woollen yarn and brushed wool together. Double crochet 1 row, turn, skip 1 stitch and double crochet back. Repeat one more time.

Edge

Change to crochet hook 3 mm and double crochet 1 row using woollen yarn, 4 ply round the cap

Mounting of lining

Cut lining according to the template Basic Design
G – Gudrun on page 55. Allow 1 cm (½ in.) for seam
allowance.
Pin the lining to the inside of the circle of felt and stitch
it on by hand.

Gitte – template

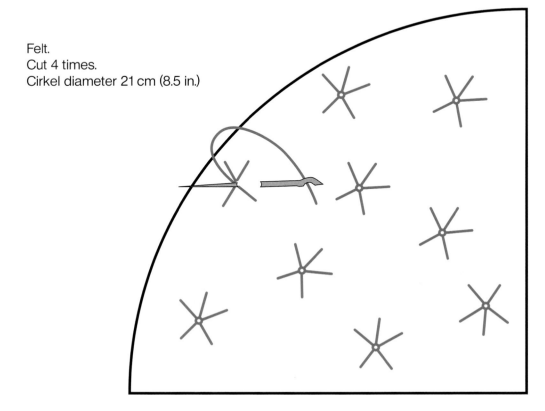

Felt.
Cut 4 times.
Cirkel diameter 21 cm (8.5 in.)

Here is a cap for windy weather as I have used wind-tight fabric for lining.

Materials

20 x 20 cm (8 x 8 in.) of felted fabric (blue shades)
100 gram woollen yarn, chunky, (denim)
A small amount of eyelash yarn (denim)
A small amount of woollen yarn, 4 ply (navy)
25 x 100 cm (10 x 40 in.) of lining
Crochet hook 6 mm
Beads

Crown

The crown is made of a circular piece of felt and a crocheted part.

Felt

Cut 4 pieces of felt according to the template Basic Design G Gitte on page 58.
Sew with woollen yarn, 4 ply, blanket stitches round the pieces of felt (Max. ½ cm, ¼ in. between stitches)
Join by overcasting in the blanket stitches so the pieces of felt form a circle.

Decoration

Embroider flowers on the circle of felt with Lazy Daisy stitches, mark the middle with beads.

Crochet

Double crochet (US single crochet).
Start crochet in the middle of the back.
Double crochet in the blanket stitches, 7 rounds with woollen yarn. Mark with contrasting yarn 10 stitches in the middle of front.
Crochet till first mark, turn and crochet back till second mark. Crochet 1 round #. Repeat # - # one more time. Crochet 5 rounds. Change to eyelash yarn and woollen yarn together, and crochet 7 rounds.

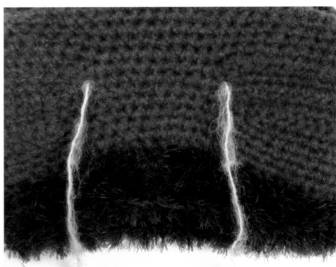

Extra decoration

Embroider flowers in front where the contrasting yarn was marking the 10 stitches. Embroider Lazy Daisy with eyelash yarn.

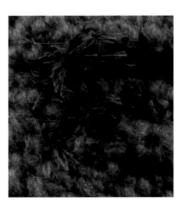

Mounting of lining

Cut and join the lining as described for Basic Design G Gretha on page 51. Pin the lining 3 cm (1 ¼ in.) above lower edge and stitch it on by hand.

Basic Design G

Gaia

It is funny to experiment with a combination of different yarns. Eyelash yarn and multicoloured sock yarn give this cap a fine play of colours.

Materials

Gaia

25 x 25 cm (10 x 10 in.) of felted fabric (bordeaux and black shades with natural white threads of silk)
80 gram multicoloured sock yarn
50 gram woollen yarn, 4 ply (bordeaux)
50 gram eyelash yarn (bordeaux)
25 x 25 cm (10 x 10 in.) of lining.
Small wooden beads
Crochet hook 3 mm

Crown

The crown is made of a circular piece of felt and a crocheted part. Since you use eyelash yarn it makes no difference crocheting in rounds or " forward and back".

Felt

Cut 4 pieces of felt according to the template Basic Design G Gitte on page 58.
Sew 120 blanket stitches round the pieces of felt (Max. ½ cm, ¼ in. between stitches)

Decoration

Embroider, with woollen yarn, rows of back stitches to indicate the lines of the felt. Embroider back stitches angled to the lines. Mark the lines further with small wooden beads.
Finally embroider small stars using back stitches spread all over the felt.

Crochet

Start crochet in the middle of the back.
Double crochet (US single crochet). 1 round in the blanket stitches. Double crochet 2 rounds using wool and sock yarn together. Crochet after that every other round with eyelash and wool yarn together, and wool and sock yarn together.
Mark with contrasting yarn (yellow) 20 stitches in the middle of the front.

Crochet till first mark, turn and crochet back till second mark. Crochet 1 round #. Repeat # - # three more times. Crochet 5 rounds.
Mark the middle of back with a safetypin, mark the 25 stitches in middle of the back. (orange yarn). These stitches are the back and you have to place the ear flaps on either sides of these stitches.

Ear flaps

Start at the orange mark, at the right side. Double crochet 15 stitches , turn , double crochet 14 stitches back. Continue decreasing 1 stitch on every row, until 5 stitches remaining. Continue double crochet 20 cm (8 in.) for string.
 Count 15 stitches before mark on left side. Make an ear flap and a string.

Edge

Double crochet 1 round with eyelash yarn.

Mounting of lining

Cut the lining according to template Basic Design G – Gudrun on page 55 and join as described for Basic Design G – Gitte on page 58.

Gunna

Basic Design G

Another nice and warm cap. The lining I have cut from a woollen scarf.

Gunna

Crown
The crown is made of a circular piece of felt and a crocheted part.

Felt
Cut the felt according to the template for Basic Design G – Gudrun on page 55
Sew 100 blanket stitches round the felt (max ½ cm, ¼ in. between stitches).

Decoration
To obtain balance in the colours and patterns of the felt, black leaves of felt are sewn on with back stitches. Afterwards the lines of the felt are outlined with rows of back stitches and black beads.

Crochet
Start crochet in the middle of the back and double crochet 1 round in the blanket stitches. Double crochet (US simgle crochet) 12 rounds with 2 threads of woollen yarn. Mark 10 stitches in the middle of front with contrasting yarn.
Double crochet till first mark, turn and crochet till second mark, double crochet 1 round #. Repeat # - # twice.

Edge
Double crochet further 8 cm (3 ¼ in.) with 2 threads of woollen yarn.
Bend 5 cm (2 in.) to the right side and stitch it to the cap.

Mounting of lining
Cut and join as described for Basic Design G – Gretha on page 51.

Hannah

Basic Design H

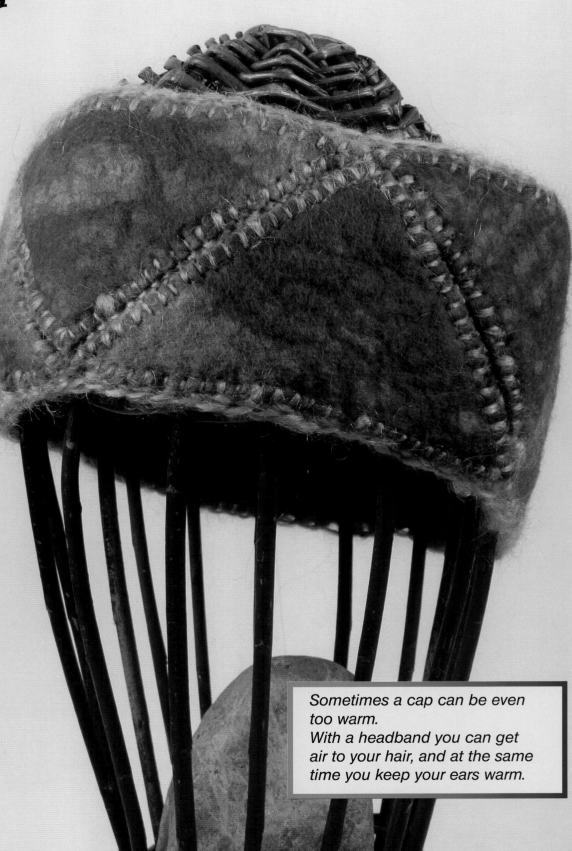

Sometimes a cap can be even too warm.
With a headband you can get air to your hair, and at the same time you keep your ears warm.

Materials

Hannah

10 x 80 cm (4 x 32 in.) of felted fabric
(cobalt and lime)
A small amount of woollen yarn 4 ply (lime)
A small amount of mohair yarn (lime)
12 x 65 cm (4¾ x 26 in.) of lining.
Elastic
Crochet hook 3 mm

Triangles of felt

Cut 8 triangles of felt according to the template on page 71.
Sew blanket stitches round each triangle. Join by overcasting in the blanket stitches, as shown on the pictures.

Double crochet 1 row in the blanket stitches at both edges, using mohair yarn.

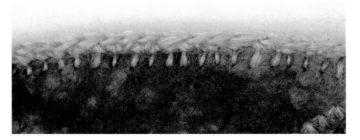

Mounting of lining

To make the width of the headband flexible you can sew on a piece of broad elastic to the wrong side of the lining.
Let the elastic measure 10 cm (4 in.), stretch it to 15 cm (6 in.) and sew the ends onto the lining. Sew 5 or 6 times at the same spot.

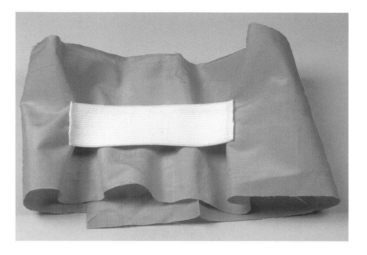

Join the lining at the short ends. Check that the width of the lining fits the headband.
Turn out the wrong side. Pin the lining to the headband and stitch it to both edges by hand.

Henriette

Basic Design H

A fairylike cap in shades
of Bordeaux-red.
It is a little funny and
has a fine fit.

Henriette

Materials

10 x 80 cm (4 x 32 in.) of felted fabric (bordeaux, black and light lilac shades, with natural white threads of silk).
50 gram woollen yarn, chunky (wine-red)
A small amount of eyelash yarn (bordeaux)
25 x 60 cm (10 x 24 in.) of lining.
Circular needle 6 mm (40 cm, 16 in.)
Double-pointed needles 6 mm
Crochet hook 6 mm
Sequins

Crown

The crown is made of a headband of felt and a knitted top.

Headband

Cut 8 triangles of felt according to the template on page 71.
Sew with chunky woollen yarn blanket stitches round each piece of felt. (max ½ cm, (¼ in.) between stitches).
Join the triangles as described for the headband on page 67

Top

Pick up 80 stitches in the blanket stitches, using circular needle 6 mm and chunky yarn.
The top is knitted in stocking stitch on circular needle. (knit all rounds).

Knit 1 round with woollen yarn.
Knit 1 round with woollen yarn and eyelash yarn together.
Knit 2 rounds with woollen yarn.
Knit 1 round with woollen yarn and eyelash yarn together
Knit 5 rounds with woollen yarn

Decrease in this way:
Knit 6 stitches, knit 2 stitches together #. Repeat # - # throughout the round.
Knit 5 rounds without decreasing.
Knit 5 stitches, knit 2 stitches together #. Repeat # - # throughout the round.
Knit 5 rounds without decreasing.
Change to double-pointed needles.

Knit 4 stitches, knit 2 stitches together #. Repeat # - # throughout the round.
Knit 3 rounds without decreasing.
Knit 3 stitches, knit 2 stitches together #. Repeat # - # throughout the round.
Knit 1 round without decreasing.
Knit 2 stitches, knit 2 stitches together #. Repeat # - # throughout the round.
Knit 1 round without decreasing.
Knit 1 stitch, knit 2 stitches together #. Repeat # - # throughout the round.
Knit 1 round without decreasing.
Knit 2 stitches together throughout the round.
Knit 5 cm (2 in.) or wanted length (The top).
Cast off and sew up.

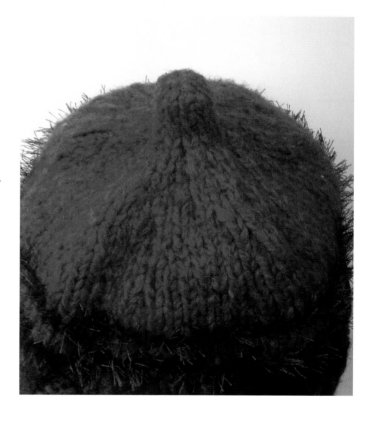

Edge

Double crochet 2 rounds with woollen yarn in every other blanket stitch at the lower edge of the headband. Double crochet (US single crochet) 1 round with eyelash yarn.

Decoration

Sew sequins onto the crocheted edge.

Mounting of lining

Cut 2 pieces of lining according to page 71, allow 1 cm,

½ in for seam allowance.

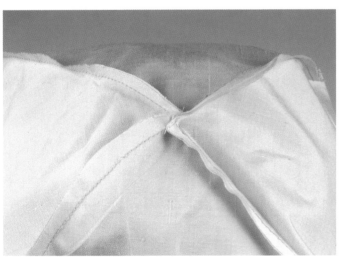

Join the lining on sewing machine. Initially join the two pieces right to the top.
Place the seams against each other and sew across.
Pin the lining to the cap and stitch it on by hand, just above the crocheted edge.

Henriette – template

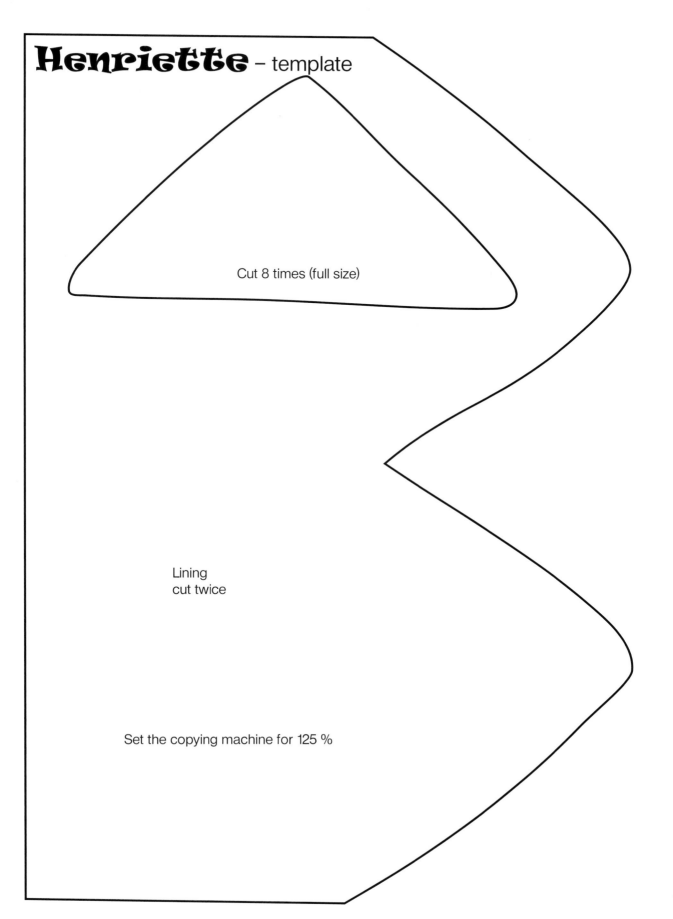

Cut 8 times (full size)

Lining
cut twice

Set the copying machine for 125 %

Helene

Basic Design H

Here is a cap which brightens up a grey winter day – a real riot of colours which makes everybody happy.

Helene

Materials
10 x 80 cm (4 x 32 in.) of felted fabric (cobalt)
50 gram multicoloured chunky yarn
A small amount of woollen yarn, 4 ply (cobalt)
25 x 60 cm (10 x 24 in.) of lining
Circular needle 6 mm (40 cm, 16 in.)
Double-pointed needles 6 mm
Crochet hook 6 mm
Sequins.

Crown

The crown is made of a headband of felt and a knitted top.

Headband

Cut 8 triangles of felt according to the template Basic Design H Henriette on page 71. Join the headband as described for design Hannah on page 67.

Top

Pick up 80 stitches, using circular needle 6 mm and multicoloured yarn, in the blanket stitches along one side.
The top is knitted in stocking stitch on circular needle. (knit all rounds).
Knit 10 rounds, and decrease in this way.
Knit 6 stitches, knit 2 stitches together #. Repeat # - # throughout the round.
Knit 5 rounds without decreasing.
Knit 5 stitches, knit 2 stitches together #. Repeat # - # throughout the round
Knit 5 rounds without decreasing.
Change to double-pointed needles 6 mm
Knit 4 stitches, knit 2 stitches together #. Repeat # - # throughout the round.
Knit 3 rounds without decreasing.
Knit 3 stitches, knit 2 stitches together #. Repeat # - # throughout the round
Knit 1 round without decreasing.
Knit 2 stitches, knit 2 stitches together #. Repeat # - # throughout the round
Knit 1 round without decreasing.
Knit 1 stitch, knit 2 stitches together #. Repeat # - # throughout the round
Knit 1 round without decreasing.
Knit 2 stitches together throughout the round.
Knit 5 cm (2 in.) or wanted length (The top).
Cast off and sew up.

Decoration

Sew sequins onto the upper edge of the headband.

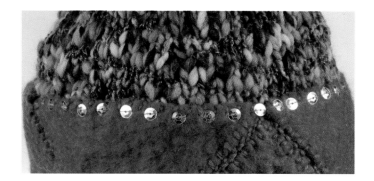

Edge

Double crochet 1 round with multicoloured yarn in the blanket stitches at the lower edge of the headband.

Mounting of lining

Cut and sew as described for Basic Design H – Henriette, page 68

Inge

Basic Design I

A knitted cap for children as well as adults. The cap is provided with lining which makes it extra warm.

Materials

75 (100) gram woollen yarn, 4 ply (green)
A small amount of woollen yarn, 4 ply (orange and yellow)
17 x 100 cm (6 ¾ x 40 in.) (19 x 120 cm (7½ x 48 in.)) of lining.
Circular needle 2 mm and 3 mm
Crochet hook 3 mm

The numbers in brackets are for adults.

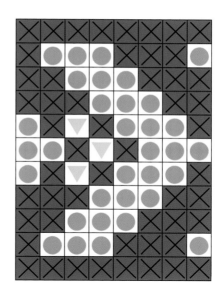

Hem

Cast on 100 (115) stitches using circular needle 2 mm and yellow yarn.
Knit 20 rounds rib (knit 1, purl 1).
Knit a round of holes for bending. # Yarn over, knit 2 stitches together #. Repeat # - #.
Knit 2 rounds in stocking stitch.

together, pass the slipped stitch over, repeat at the other marks.
Change to double-pointed needles when necessary.
Continue untill 2 stitches remain on every needle.
Cut yarn, leaving long end, and thread through the remaining stitches.
Gather up and fasten securely.

Outside of hem and crown

Change to needle 3 mm and green yarn. Increase on first round till 112 (136) stitches.
Knit 22 rounds, knit pattern from chart. Continue with green yarn till work measures 16 (18) cm (6½ (7¼) in.) from the round of holes.
Mark 4 "corners" with contrasting yarn, 28 (34) stitches between marks. Decrease on every round in this way:
Slip 1 stitch before mark, move mark, knit 2 stitches

Tassels

Make four tassels:
Wrap orange yarn loosely around a piece of cardboard.
Thread a strand (or more) of yarn through the top and tie firmly with a square knot, leaving a long end (min. 30 cm, 12 in.) for later.

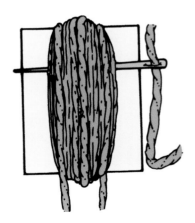

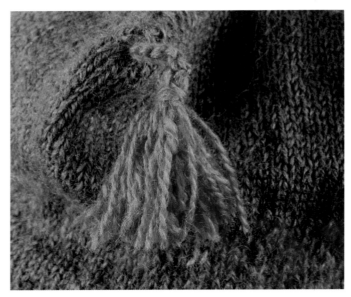

Cut the strands at the bottom.

Mounting of lining

Bend the hem and stitch it loosely to the wrong side of the cap.
Cut a piece of lining measuring 17 x 17 cm (20 x 20 cm) 6 ¾ x 6 ¾ in. (8 in. 8 in.) and a piece measuring 17 x 70 cm (19 x 100 cm) 6 ¾ x 28 in. (7½ x 40 in.) Join the largest piece into a tube and sew on sewing machine. Divide into four and place a pin. Join the other piece of lining to the marks as a crown and sew.
Pin the lining to the cap and stitch it on by hand right above the hem.

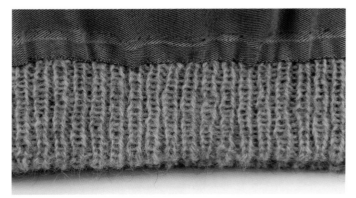

Hide the knot, and the short end left from tying it, under the folded strands.
Wind the long strand a few times to secure the folded end, then tread it through so that it comes out at the top and chrochet 5 chain stitches. Trim ends.
Sew tassels onto the cap at the "corners"

Basic Design J

This knitted cap is very warm and therefore perfect for skiing and toboggan rides. The design is suitable for both women and men.

Jane

Jane

Knit till work measures 18 cm (7 ¼ in.) from edge. Mark with contrasting yarn 4 times, 30 stitches between marks. Decrease at marks on every other round in this way: Slip 1 stitch, knit 2 together, pass slipped stitch over. Change to double-pointed needles when necessary. Continue decreasing till 8 stitches remain (14 decreases in all) .

Cut yarn, leaving long end, and thread through the remaining stitches. Gather up and fasten securely.

Rolling edge

Cast on 120 stitches using angora yarn and circular needle 2 mm.
Knit 6 rounds of stocking stitch.

Tassels

Make 3 tassels according to the instruction at Basic Design I – Inge , page 76. (Leave longer ends, (about 50 cm, 20 in.)

Strings for the tassels

Crochet, using the ends, respectively 15, 18 and 22 chain stitches. Hereby the strings will get different lengths. Sew the tassels securely to the top of the cap.

Crown

Change to circular needle 3 mm and grey woollen yarn.
Knit 6 rounds and continue with pattern from chart.
Continue making the crown.

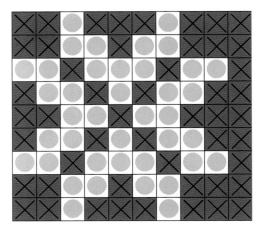

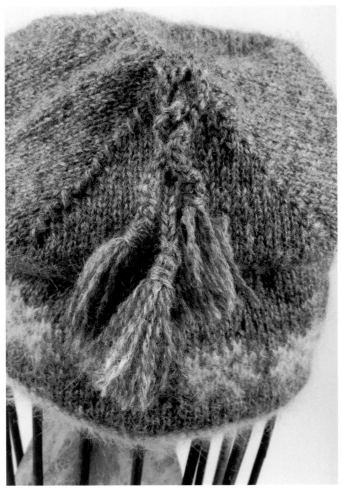

Edge inside the cap

Pick up 120 stitches in purl loops inside the cap, right above the rolling edge, using wool and angora yarn on circular needle 2 mm.
Knit 7 cm (2 ¾ in.) (stocking stitch). Cast off loosely.
Stitch the inside edge to the cap by hand.

Mounting of lining

Cut lining according to template for Basic Design H – Henriette on page 71. Join according to the instruction on page 70.